*Tender Light Softens*

# *Tender Light Softens*

## When the Deep Places Speak

### Sarah Carlson

2022
GOLDEN DRAGONFLY PRESS
AMHERST, MASSACHUSETTS

FIRST PRINT EDITION, October 2022
FIRST EBOOK EDITION, November 2022

Copyright © 2022 by Sarah Carlson
All rights reserved.
Set in Scrivano and Adobe Garamond Pro.

Cover photograph by © Sarah Carlson
Photography by © Sarah Carlson
Photographs for the Dedication, Author's photo, Preface, *Remember*, *Upheld* and *I'll Hold You, Too* by © Emma Carlson.
Artwork for *The Closing, The Opening* was a gift from a fourth-grade student.

No part of this publication may be reproduced or transmitted in any form or by any means, electronic or otherwise, without prior written permission by the copyright owner.

ISBN: 978-1-7370545-3-5

Printed on acid-free paper supplied by a Forest Stewardship Council-certified provider. First published in the United States of America by Golden Dragonfly Press, 2022.

www.meanderingsoftheheart.blogspot.com

www.goldendragonflypress.com

*In memory of Barry Francis Carlson*

*Dedicated to our grandson, Otto,
who, simply by being his sweet self, helps us remember:*

### Let It Sing

Drop in. Listen.
Allow the flow
from within.
Let the deep places speak—
from you, for you,
with you.
Notice what surfaces
as it swirls, sifts
and then settles
just as you need
it to be.
In those moments
your heart sings a song
of you.
So drop in, listen
and let it sing.

August 1, 2016

# Contents

| | |
|---|---|
| *Preface* | xi |
| The Delicacy of Softening | 1 |
| Tender Magic | 2 |
| In and Above | 3 |
| Gentle Power of Health | 5 |
| My Voice | 6 |
| Tender Light Softens | 8 |
| To Our Children | 9 |
| The Peace of the Pines | 11 |
| Togetherness | 13 |
| The Flooding and the Freeing | 15 |
| To the Moon | 16 |
| The Grief of Isolation | 18 |
| When the Deep Places Speak | 20 |
| Pandemic Peace | 22 |
| The Light of Love, Too | 24 |
| Rejuvenation | 26 |
| Dear, Sweet, Beautiful Self | 27 |
| At Home | 29 |
| Let Go the Disquiet | 30 |
| This Poetic Me | 32 |
| Let You Be at Peace | 34 |
| On a Clear Day | 35 |
| Allow the Clouds | 37 |

| | |
|---|---|
| A World Askew Quiets | 39 |
| My Mother's Garden | 40 |
| In Between | 42 |
| 4 Roberts Avenue | 43 |
| Above | 45 |
| Novel Ways to Shine | 47 |
| Celestial Energy | 48 |
| In the Depths of You | 50 |
| Pause | 52 |
| The Closing, The Opening | 54 |
| Thank You… | 56 |
| Ocean Dance | 58 |
| A Subtle Shift | 59 |
| Spread Your Light | 61 |
| Deep Simplicity | 62 |
| Peace in the Pieces | 63 |
| My Brother's Stone | 65 |
| A Softness to This Day | 66 |
| The Adventure of Being Human | 68 |
| Upheld | 69 |
| Widen | 71 |
| Even a Little Bit of Light | 72 |
| Years and Years of Tears | 73 |
| In the Waning | 75 |
| Slow Motion | 76 |
| Solstice in the Wings | 78 |
| The Vast Reaches of You | 79 |
| Newness | 81 |
| Singular | 82 |
| Such Illumination | 84 |
| The Energy of it All | 86 |
| What's True | 87 |
| In the Glistening | 89 |
| Thank you, Father | 90 |

| | |
|---|---|
| This Light of Mine | 91 |
| Unbounded | 93 |
| A Pandemic Year | 94 |
| Through the Heart of a Teacher | 94 |
| Mommy…Where's God? | 96 |
| Moments Such as This | 98 |
| Solace | 99 |
| Salty Softness | 100 |
| Finding Oneself in Solitude | 102 |
| I'll Hold You, Too | 103 |
| Smothered No Longer | 105 |
| Held | 106 |
| The Fullness of Grief | 108 |
| Ever More | 109 |
| Unburdened | 111 |
| This Day | 113 |
| Freshening | 114 |
| The Me That He Sees | 116 |
| When the Doing is Done | 117 |
| In the Company of Love | 119 |
| Bear Witness | 120 |
| Crisis | 122 |
| Reveal | 124 |
| This Bold Love | 126 |
| Thank You, Blue Heron | 127 |
| Divinely They Dance | 129 |
| Baptism by Nature | 130 |
| Wide-eyed Wonder | 132 |
| Of Sunshine and Raindrops | 133 |
| Collected Sorrow | 135 |
| Because I Am In It | 136 |
| Led by Light | 138 |
| In and Around and Above | 140 |
| The Calm Comfort of Love | 141 |

| | |
|---|---|
| A Sense of Place Within | 143 |
| Step Into the Storm | 145 |
| Anew | 146 |
| Tender Light Softens, Still | 148 |
| A Hope-Finder | 149 |
| Illumine | 151 |
| Wake More Fully to Beauty | 152 |
| The Broken Can Blossom | 153 |
| The Quiet Beauty of You | 155 |
| Sacred Fog | 156 |
| The Power of Love | 159 |
| As Wide as the Ocean | 161 |
| Fostering Hope | 162 |
| Out There | 164 |
| Found | 166 |
| Quiet Currents | 168 |
| Remember | 170 |
| *Other Books by Sarah* | 173 |

# Preface

**LOVE**—A WONDERFUL WORD, intricate idea, beautiful belief, that when freely shared spreads warmth, tenderness, and light throughout.

I have learned so much in the 20 years since the man I loved passed away very suddenly one beautiful spring day. This includes understanding that Love is unique to those who share it and can be wide, palpable, and sustaining even when one's physical presence is no longer. I'm not here to say that it is an easy process to explore the sorrows that loss contains. I am here to say that tensions harbored within, whatever their origin, can transform into wellness and movement toward wholeness. The poems in this book reflect exploring those sorrows with healthy doses of hope, which has lead to experiencing the comfort of Love more and more deeply. Along the way, tender light does soften over and over again.

My husband, Barry, died while doing something he absolutely loved—playing tennis with good friends. Just a few days earlier, we had spent some family time along the river that flows near our home. We had walked to our special spot under the light of a full moon, which shimmered from one bank to the other. Two Canada geese landed in that reflected light. We talked later about how spiritual those moments had been and how we considered nature to be our temple. To this day, I remain grateful for that conversation. And for the light that glittered in the darkness.

I was not a stranger to grief, having lost my only sibling in a bicycling accident in 1987 when he was 33, just days before my 30th birthday. Fifteen years later, as I began to attend to the heartache of losing my soulmate, I somehow knew that I needed to go into the sorrow, that there was much to learn and opportunity to grow. Those moments with the geese opened my mind and my heart to noticing how I felt as I walked, paddled, pedaled, and skied— alone or with family and friends. I would find myself pausing and settling while watching clouds, spotting birds, examining the play of light on water, finding heart rocks at the most opportune times. I often took photos of those serendipitous scenes.

Though I have always enjoyed writing, often wrote poetry as a child, and had a literature minor as I pursued a teaching degree, I did not formally study the writing of poetry. Yet, a poetic voice emerged and needed to be recognized as part of my healing process. Before long, I realized that my writings and photographs were linked, and so I began pairing them together. I published my first book, *The Radiance of Change*, independently in early 2018. The second, *In the Currents of Quiet*, made its way into my hands just as COVID-19 began to take hold. The poems in this collection range in time from just before the pandemic (December 2019) through August 2022. Sometimes it has felt odd to be accessing so much healing through a time that has been fraught with unease and confusion all around the world. At the same time, though, it actually does make sense.

We humans have dealt with a great deal as we navigate COVID-19. All while experiencing everyday life as it unfolds. For me, that has included walking out of my fourth-grade classroom on March 13, 2020, not realizing I would never return to teaching as I knew it. Along with that came learning that my first grandchild was on the way, the decline and death of my intrepid 96-year-old mother just a few weeks later, cleaning out my childhood home as the only member of my nuclear family still here—a home that my parents had owned for over 60 years. The contents of the house included my father's ashes. Though we had a memorial service for him after he died in 2011, my mother chose to keep him close to her. So, I planned an outdoor COVID-safe interment of both their ashes in the summer of 2020. Somewhere in there, I took a hard fall mountain biking that resulted in a concussion. I also made the difficult decision to retire from a profession I truly loved so I could be in my grandchild's COVID baby bubble when he arrived in October 2020. Shortly after I retired, I was asked if I would consider teaching in a newly-formed remote academy that my district developed in response to the pandemic. I did so willingly and proceeded to work harder than ever to make sure, with my co-teacher, that the 40 or so students in our care received the best fourth-grade education we could provide. And, I was still able to be in that wonderful bubble as Oma for my adorable grandson, Otto.

One of the most profound experiences of publishing my first book happened in my fourth-grade classroom. I had shared the process with my class and they were so excited when I finally had the book in my hands. I put one in our classroom library in case they wanted to explore it. Not long after that, several families purchased a copy at our local bookstore. One morning, to my surprise, I looked up and saw that six students had MY book open for quiet reading time. That led to a conversation later in the day with a young man who quietly confided in me that he, his mom, and his brother were reading some poems each night. His dad had died a few years earlier and he told me it was helping them talk about that loss as a family. That's just one example of how my story and sharing it through poetry and photography opens the way for others to explore and share their own.

And it is the sharing of our stories, I believe, that is the path to a more authentically linked community—especially these days when so much hovers on the surface in our social media oriented world. Poetry is a beautifully effective way to capture the moments in life when a deep connection happens. It is also an opportunity to play with words and the rhythm of language, to set listeners, readers, and writers free to explore inner tempos and let their unique hearts sing. And that's when the magic of connection reveals, unfolds, and paves the way anew.

I write these pieces, take these photos, as I meander my way through all that life contains for an open-hearted human. Though they deal with loss, they are full of growth, promise, healing, and light. I share them with love and the hope that they may touch readers' lives in such a way as to be of comfort or inspiration or even a chance to let whatever emotions that may arise freely flow.

I remain grateful to the people with whom I continue to process and share, discover and heal:

Daniel Gibbons, D.O. Jonathan M. Borkum, Ph.D. The Reverend Ann Kidder M. Div., S.T.M.

I'd like to thank Angela Werner of Höhne-Werner Design, from whom I learned so much during the publishing of the first two books and who again has been a gentle guide with putting this one together by helping me with the editing. I am grateful to Alice Maldonado of Golden Dragonfly Press for the opportunity to publish through her press.

I am extremely appreciative of the readers of my work, both the ones I've heard from or shared with and those who have held books in their hands without my knowing.

I also feel honored to have spent a great deal of time over the years with natural poets—children, both my own, and 31 years worth of students. They helped nurture the voice that simply had to be heard and has made its way onto the pages of my books.

I'm grateful to my parents for bringing my brother and me into this world and for fostering a love of the outdoors in both of us. And, of course, I'm so happy that I had 27 years with a man who saw me for me, for the two wonderful children we had together, for their spouses who fill their lives with even more love, and for my little grandson, Otto—who helps us all remember to look closely, listen intently, and love deeply.

# The Delicacy of Softening

Life lesions leave some parts of us
splintered, spiky, silenced.
As those places awaken,
begin to speak,
we must listen with care,
for they have much to teach.
A toughness
may have barricaded them,
formed as necessary protection
from the causes
and effects.
This barrier likely has intricate facets.
As it loosens,
gentleness and kindness
to oneself
are vital.
Inner awareness,
faith in relationship,
belief in one's validity,
are strong company
for the wonder of revival.
As those once sharp, stiff,

broken places
mellow and mend,
one can appreciate and welcome
the delicacy of softening.

January 16, 2020

## Tender Magic

Moments
when the bounty of love
flows free and true,
around and through.
They can peel away layers,
sculpt newness,
allow ease,
provide equilibrium.
What a wondrous sensation
relaxing into
these currents of health
can be.
A pause, a breath,
a time of noticing
what is

right there, right then.
Later,
in times of duress
when pain may come into play,
one can revive
the tender magic
of those moments.
Beautiful blessings
freely available to those
who choose to savor
their soulful significance,
allow them to be an antidote
to whatever may cause distress.

January 26, 2020

## In and Above

There's health in noticing
an imbalance within,
especially when paired with
a recognition of the solidity
with which one has thrived
in previous precarious predicaments.

There's a tippy-ness
to inward rearrangement
until one gazes up and out.
Just as a waxing moon
can both nestle in
and orbit above
the bare branches of a singular tree,
so can one burrow
and rise.
Gently,
constantly,
palpably,
progress occurs
inward and overhead.
Such sweetness
in pausing to notice
the strength of the shifting,
the grace of the glow,
the power of the potential
to be
in and above
at the very same time.

February 6, 2020

# Gentle Power of Health

She sits quietly listening,
then ponders, offers, reflects.
With deep empathy
her presence is true.
Embedded in her substance,
it becomes part of her healing
to acknowledge within.
This multi-layered understanding
enlightens a deep, achy place
that speaks plainly
of having witnessed words
used as vehicles of hurt
instead of transporting love.
Caring, listening hearts
were not always available
in her times of need,
but she can speak safely now,
believe in their presence,
take in benevolence
and support.
She knows her tippy-ness
will remedy
as re-balancing
takes hold in her now.
She smiles,
feels the warm,
gentle power of health.
Compassion for her
own veritable being,
including those places that ache,
wends its way throughout.
Though connection
with others is important,

something she still
often craves,
she enfolds her being,
taking time to care for and about
her kindhearted self.

February 8, 2020

# My Voice

I found it a while ago.
It's right here on this page,
has proven to be a trusty craft.
I've listened to it, honored it,
let it interleave in my healing.
I've explored and expressed
inner fronds of dark and light
and everything in between.
And yet sometimes
when it is the spoken word,
when I say what I feel, think, need,
there's the possibility of
constriction still.
I wonder,

"Am I complaining,
talking out of turn,
saying anything hurtful or …
wrong?"
My belly begins to ache
and I feel a twitchy energy
that doesn't resonate with now.
Then I realize that I deserve
to speak.
I didn't deserve
to be stifled—
ever.
My voice is filled
with care, concern, curiosity.
My words are
sincere, sweet, sonorous.
When I speak and write,
I allow light out from within
and in from without.
There's no reason to hold it back.
My voice—
a means of expression
of the magic
of me.

February 20, 2020

## Tender Light Softens

Frozen layers underfoot
gleam in softened beams
that reach from
fading sun to
woodsy trails.
Skiers slow to a stop,
breathe,
take it all in.
Tranquil tree shadows
stretch in the gentle glow
as dark and light mingle.

In times of sorrow and unease
remember to notice,
honor, welcome
glimmers of brightness
wherever, whenever
they appear.
The act of slowing
allows the opportunity
to treasure the truth
as tender light

spreads to the places that need
the warmth of its benevolence
the most.
Inner tensions again unwind
as muscles relax,
cells open,
blood flows.
Though sorrow and unease
are discernible,
tender light softens,
illuminates hope and healing
as they sink, soothe,
and circulate.

March 4, 2020

## To Our Children

We love you.
The questions you have right now
make sense.
It's okay to wonder and ask.

As teachers, family, friends,
we are answering as best we can.
We understand
that you want those answers
to be clear and true.
Sometimes we adults
just have to calmly say,
"I'm not sure,
but here's what we know."
And even that changes
from day to day.

Remember that there are things
we do know for sure.
The solid earth is still spinning
so that the sun rises
to greet each new day.
Our majestic moon moves
through its predictable
and lovely phases.
Beautiful cloud formations
come and go
as varied winds blow.
So, whenever you feel unsure,
raise your gaze to the sky,
take a breath,
notice the beauty
of the natural world.
Look into the eyes
of someone you love
and just be
in that moment.
Open a book and
let its story unfold.
Grab a pencil
and let yours do the same.

And, don't forget—
we adults who are your teachers,
family, and friends—
WE LOVE YOU.

March 14, 2020

## The Peace of the Pines

Setting out into the woods
she slides one foot in front of the other,
finds a tentative rhythm
on the changing surface.
She decides to climb
to the top of the ridge,
skis a few loops
as anxious tensions release,
replaced by the pleasure of
physical exertion and
self-locomotion.
Reluctant to head back down,
once more she makes her way to the top,
recognizes a gentle knowing
that's drawing her there.

Pausing in the familiar stand of pines,
she allows her breath and heart to settle.
She watches and listens
as sun-kissed trees sway
in diverse winds
against the backdrop
of a brilliant blue sky.
In the sights and sounds of winter woods,
understanding slowly comes
and the heaviness of collective sadness
lightens a bit.
She takes a deep breath,
smiles and remembers
that, as always, Nature knows.
Though each tree stands separate and singular,
their roots hold the ground together.
Isolation and connection
right there in front of her eyes.
Filled with the wisdom of the woods,
the peace of the pines,
she gratefully, gallantly
turns toward home.

March 15, 2020

# Togetherness

The rhythm of our seasons,
the dance of sun and Earth,
the interplay of dark and light.

We started school as summer was ending
and the Autumnal Equinox approached.
We got to know each other,
found our rhythms in our classrooms—
together.
Leaves changed and so did we.
Daylight dwindled,
with Winter Solstice
a time to notice
and celebrate the dark of night,
the promise of growing light.
Our cadence became stronger as community grew
and our minds and hearts did, too.
Slowly, day by day, light has expanded
as snow melts, trees awaken,
birds chirp their springtime songs.
The Vernal Equinox is here,
we welcome it
apart from each other.
Days will continue to lengthen,
trees will bud,
flowers begin to find their way
into the warm sunshine.

In this time of uncertainty
and lack of physical contact,
let us all remember that
we are connected.
May we look to the sky, the earth,

and to each other.
May we savor moments
with family and friends
in any way that we can.
May we be happy,
may we be safe,
may we feel love
all around and through us.
May we allow our emotions
and take comfort
in predictable patterns
like the changing seasons.
May we be open to experiencing
togetherness
in new and creative ways
as we work our way through
these tricky times.

March 20, 2020

# The Flooding and the Freeing

Fortifying liquid flows
around, through, and in.
A flood,
but with a power that is
gentle and comfortable and right.
Surface sparkles sink in,
travel to far reaches,
ignite ever more fully that which
has long been kindled.
Detritus that had collected
along the shores
and in varied nooks
wobbles in the waves,
then cleanly clears away.
Pure, wholesome waters glide,
as a soft breeze delivers
promise, truth, newness.
A twitch, a breath,
a release, a remembering,
a coming together within.
Body fills with tender recognition
of pristine, cohesive pieces of self.
Misty, mindful eyes marvel at
a pulsating mosaic of colors as
those pieces re-combine and align.
Soul expands without encumbrance
from solid ground
to lofty stars
and back again.
Circuit completes with
a fresh, relaxing, full breath

as the flooding softly
gives way
to freedom.

March 25, 2020

## To the Moon

Your presence is so steady,
your phases predictable,
your comings and goings
such a delight.
You have the power to pull tides,
shift energies,
reflect the sun's light.
Your patterns
have a quiet,
soothing majesty.
Sometimes being with you
is especially profound,
resonates deeply,
both within and without.

On a familiar hilltop she waits,

wonders where you are
as she anticipates your full rising.
She sees the low clouds,
but doesn't realize
how dense they are
until your vibrant light emerges,
higher in the sky than expected.
She breathes, sighs, settles.
As you slowly make your way
into the twilight sky
she feels her own light expand
with yours
as inner clouds disperse.
You gently tug her heartstrings,
allowing antiquated pulls to lessen.
She breathes, sighs, settles even more.
With one more look
she gratefully
turns toward home,
your light,
her light,
leading her
tenderly there.

April 9, 2020

# The Grief of Isolation

First off, I do know
that I am not fully alone.
I get it, I really do.
However,
in these days and weeks,
now likely to be months,
of the physical distancing
of Covid 19,
I am isolated,
spend much of my time solo.
A widow,
one who has worked hard
to explore and learn from
the many facets of loss,
the grief of not having him here
is true.
A mother,
who did her best to be present
with our children
after his death,
there is grief to what
shifted between us.

A teacher,
one who thrives
on the inlets and outlets
of sharing in a classroom community,
there is grief in not being with students,
to being unsure as to how to find a new flow.
A sister,
whose brother died long ago.
A daughter,
whose father is gone
and whose mother can barely see.
A poet,
with a book full of her love
and healing,
that now sits in boxes with
nowhere to go.
All these pieces and more
are mine,
are part of me.
There is deep grief present.
I will sit with it, learn from it,
partner it with gratitude for all that is good.
But, I had to name it.
It's real and strong,
just like me.
I'll be okay,
but deep grief
is definitely present.

April 10, 2020

# When the Deep Places Speak

Awakenings—
when things open and unfurl,
fueled by the warmth of
nurturing, golden light
from above and around
and within.
Surfaces and cells
stretch, soften,
give voice to all
that has been and
needs acknowledgment
in the now.
Some things,
long forgotten,
may seep to the surface
or adhere from outside.
This may ache,
cause some quivers,
or the need to cry away.
There will likely be grief
from things known
and things not.

Another opportunity
to sit in stillness,
let come what may,
allow it into
the light of day.
No need to carry,
or hold on,
or be held back
any longer.
No need to worry,
judge,
allow concocted wrongness
to infiltrate.
Roots hold fast,
purity flows,
love supports and embraces
when those powerful and pure
deep places speak.

April 7–17, 2020

## Pandemic Peace

Deep, deep breaths,
in … out … in … out … in … out.
Within the solid walls of your home,
and the linear edges of your computer screen,
settle into the soft
surrounds of your body.
If your mind is at first busy,
appreciate your amazing ability to think.
Then, allow thoughts to fade or rise
or flow away.
Relax your eyebrows and behind your eyes.
Let that sense of ease slide down to your jaw
as you allow it to slacken.
Downward into your neck,
comfort seeps to your shoulders
as muscles slowly and surely,
softly, ever so softly, settle.
Now …
drop into your heart space,
that place where you really are.
Feel the expansiveness
of love … and compassion,

as they gently swirl
in and around and through.
Sit with this for a bit,
giving quiet a chance to widen.

As you let your time of stillness
come to an end,
imagine this love and compassion
that resides in your heart space
as a golden glow.
Feel it warm you from within,
while at the very same time you
let it wend its way
into the reality of the room where you are,
the virtual space we share,
the wider world
where all of us everywhere
can feel its smooth and silky support.
May we feel this love in tandem.
May we embrace this compassion as a community.
May we allow this peace that can be found
in these currents of quiet
that flow from our hearts
to buoy us and sustain us
as we navigate this pandemic together.

April 18, 2020

# The Light of Love, Too

Freedom comes as one opens
to the Light of Love
without reservation or defense.
Its branches and tendrils,
currents and vapors,
are both earthbound
and lofty.
It is ready and available
for giving and receiving,
for the conduit to be complete.

Vulnerable infant,
wide-eyed toddler,
sweet little girl,
anxious teen …
For all those years love
flowed naturally from her
into her world.
It was reciprocated,
but not always by those
who were the receivers,
so she wondered and worried

that perhaps she did not deserve.
Then, her life and his merged
and she couldn't help but let
the strength of his love in.
It was truly undeniable.
It provided an anchor and she relaxed
in the flow of marriage, motherhood, and teaching.
Tragedy struck and she became
adrift and unsure once more,
though love still emanated from within.
Her natural propensity to care for others
remained strong,
while the sense of possible unworthiness
again took hold in a deep, familiar place.
Choosing to explore her fathoms,
over time she has learned to let go of the pulls,
release the tensions,
allow the full, deep breath
of Spirit to enter,
restore, revitalize.
Slowly, steadily
she internalizes
that she really does deserve
that Light of Love, too.
Nothing to do
other than continue
to learn to allow it
to manifest and bolster
her innate vitality.

April 21, 2020

# Rejuvenation

Roots hold fast,
pull nourishment from
the awakening ground.
Limbs softly sway,
reach into the warmth
and glow of the wide open sky.
Inner world enlivens
as trunk aligns,
joints and cells settle
right where they need to be.
A breath, a stretch, a gaze above.
Traumatic tensions
from a long, cold winter
wisp away,
replaced by peaceful currents
of growth and hope.
Though winter held a beauty all its own
and much was gleaned
from its presence,
the time has come
for rejuvenation.

May 5, 2020

# Dear, Sweet, Beautiful Self

She breathes deep the gathering bloom,
pushes through the ground,
straightens and
opens to the light of day.
She relishes the feel of
sunlight on her skin,
breezes on her face,
orienting of her cells
to newness.
Even under the cold weight
of grief,
she feels her strength
and kindness
and empathetic nature.
She knows these will help her
attend to her own needs.
It is heavy,
this grief.
It has many angles and facets,
twists and turns,
faces and memories.
And, it surely is

a strange time
to experience all this.
A time when there are
other forms of grief
in the here and now.
And so she pauses
and breathes,
slowly acknowledges
that she must allow it to be,
that it will melt or flow or wisp away
when the time is right.
It may make her bend,
cause some distress,
but she knows
she will not break.
She must take time,
be patient and kind
with her dear, sweet,
beautiful self.

May 9, 2020

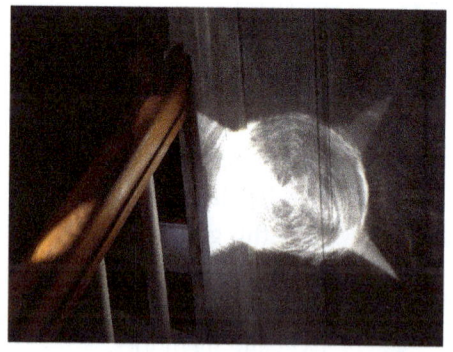

# At Home

Sorting through a house that
often didn't feel much
like a home.
Loaded layers,
varied valuables,
records of ruin,
random, self-serving journals.
Loving, caring, compassionate me.
Gently present as I always have been,
making sense of a tangled mess
that, once unraveled,
reveals truths.
Some that I knew all along,
others that have
an exciting novelty.
The most important is—
I am safely
at home
in me.
And, with that on board,
I can forgive,
feel grateful,
tap ever more deeply into
the Light of Love.
My own gentle presence
lovingly settles
into the amazing experience
of being safely
at home
in me.

June 2, 2020

# Let Go the Disquiet

Her nose wrinkles,
head aches,
chest tightens,
and then something shadowy
that does not have,
or need,
clear definition,
goes.
Though wispy and nebulous,
it has a pungent mustiness,
a stale sense of
foreboding.
It curls away in a smoky haze,
taking with it that
which never really did belong
to her.
So much harbored in its layers
wounded her,
and she needs reassurance that
it cannot, will not
hurt anyone else,
ever.

Her wonder-filled wild child
needs to know,
and she's learned to ask
or name or speak
instead of holding on,
holding in,
particularly in this time
of grief and upheaval
within her being
and in the wider world.
She feels a deep sense of promise
as her beautiful body balances
and she slowly, gently
lets go the disquiet,
hands it over to the Divine,
once again breathes in the
fresh, clean breezes
of release, renewal,
and rejuvenation.

June 3, 2020

# This Poetic Me

Familiar scenes experienced
through an ever-changing lens.
Opportunities to explore
that which happened long ago
from the perspective of health.
The unwinding
of a very complex ravel
without having to analyze
every part of the weave.
A sense of gratitude
for things kept hidden away,
though for reasons not fully known,
to be found by a daughter
lovingly sorting through it all.
Correspondence between
a brother and a sister,
dated September 1964,
hinting at the brokenness
between them.
Journals written by a mother
infused with deep despair,
detailed descriptions of disquiet.

Letters brimming
with wisdom and love,
from an 18, 19, 20-year-old me.
All revealing the validity
of my memories, sensations,
bygone distress.
Sweetly sinking into
a gentle realigning,
a truly novel
sense of balance,
mingled with a recognition
that reflections
don't have to be fully clear
to allow for the
peace of understanding
and the safety of self.
This deep dive into what was
verifies the reasons
for my careful explorations,
upholds the exquisite grace
of the images and insights
that emerge from
this poetic me.

June 13, 2020

## Let You Be at Peace

You left so much
for me to sort through.
It's been a challenge,
but more importantly,
a gift.
It helped me see
that what I remember is true.
The tug of the house
and all it contained was strong,
but the energy of love
has more vigor, warmth,
and radiance.
I knew to follow it,
have done so with
courage and tenacity
that also comes from you.
And so, Mom and Dad,
now it's time for me
to let you be at peace.
Rest together,
as the struggles
really are over.

Know that I love you,
always have, always will.
I know you love me, too.
You have my gratitude
and my hope that you
settle into Grace,
be with Love,
rest in Peace.

Love, Sarah
June 25, 2020

## On a Clear Day

Sliding once again into
restorative, silky waters
she lays back,
allows natural buoyancy to
hold her steady and balanced.
So many beautiful words
have flowed through her
and into the world.
She knows they represent

the truth of healing.
With a profound realization
that she had to fully trust
her own memories
of the wound
to deeply embody
those truths,
she again feels something
novel and familiar.
She feels herself.
All the way in,
all the way out.
No need to apologize
or try so very hard.
That's what's happening now—
unlearning the constant sense
that there must be effort
to earn
the right
to be who she is.
Letting go the habit of
waiting with bated breath
to see if she made a mistake
or failed.
Trusting the clarity that's present
on a clear day,
while knowing clouds
will come and go,
but that she didn't cause the clouds.
They are simply there
and will pass.
She can and will continue
to settle more and more
into the comfort and safety
of being
at home

in herself.
On those clear days,
any day really,
it's okay to simply be.

June 18, 2020

## Allow the Clouds

We all know that clouds
come and go.
Sometimes when they
have settled low on the horizon,
they have the potential
to be a bit smothering,
though the waters below
are no less silky.
Their denseness may temporarily
overpower the ease and warmth
of lightness within,
so it is important
to remember that eventually,
no matter what,
they do drift away

with changing winds.
With these understandings aboard
it becomes easier to
allow the clouds
to be whatever, however
they are.
There is always light
above them, behind them.
Whether it be the twinkling stars
and glowing moon of night,
or the gleaming sun of day,
the truth of Light
is undeniable.
If we do
allow the clouds,
we discover
they, too,
have a necessary
validity
and there is ease
to embracing it all.

June 23, 2020

# A World Askew Quiets

Stepping into clear waters,
she disrupts the surface,
makes it ripple a bit.
Unsettled sunbeams
wiggle and dance
as her toes sink slightly
into soft sand.
Gratefully, she fills her lungs,
smiles with simple delight,
starts her gentle morning swim
as cavorting light continues.
Her mind drifts with wonder
at how chaos and calm
can occupy
the very same space,
images of those interweaving beams
amplifying her awareness.
Buoyant body relaxes,
energy aligns,
spirit enlivens.
The buzzing energy of
a world askew quiets
and she settles ever more deeply
into her lively, loving home.

June 25, 2020

# My Mother's Garden

She devised a seemingly beautiful space
inside our home.
But, it was outside
where the real beauty took hold.
An open field
that gradually became
a meandering garden,
with trees for shade
and places to rest.
She created it over time,
a place for her respite and delight.
I tried to join her there,
but we were usually going
in conflicting directions.
At least that's how it felt.
Occasionally,
our paths would merge,
but it was brief
and I couldn't seem to match her step,
perhaps wasn't meant to.
I knew to follow love,
even came back to be married there.

The last time I talked with my brother
was right there, too.
The disjointed, confusing
energy of the place
has been present throughout.
But now as I prepare
to fully walk away,
I can more freely reap the benefits
of other seeds that were sown.
Athleticism, strength, courage,
ability to find hope, no matter what.
I have those with me, too.
I can recognize and allow the blossoms
of my mother's garden.
I can be me right where I am.
I don't have to be
there anymore.

July 3, 2020

# In Between

A bridge goes from one side
to another.
From here to there.
Yet, when you get there,
it's actually a new here
and onward you go.
I've been thinking lately
that the spans of bridges actually
have something to teach.
Marvels of engineering,
it is those spans where
the true magic resides
as they miraculously
bear the load.
I think it wise to
pause on a bridge
every so often,
take a look at what's going on
below, within, above.
Whether a bridge
crosses some muck
on a woodsy trail,

carries you across
flowing waters,
takes you over a path
that leads somewhere else,
there's something soothing about
suspending in the moments
of in-between
and being
right where you are.

July 10, 2020

# 4 Roberts Avenue

My address from birth to 18.
The key was 'hidden' on the second shelf
of a corner cupboard in the breezeway.
On the left was the door
to the funky garage that housed
Merry Meeting Black Jack's kennel
and my brother's darkroom,
but never, ever had room for a car.
Breezeway and funky garage
no longer exist,

except in my memories,
replaced by a large entryway
and not-quite-finished addition.
On the right was the door to the kitchen,
once a sort of disjointed affair,
but redone, made more open in 1971.
The wonderful screened-in back porch
became a lovely sunroom in 1986,
but the rest of the home didn't
change much over the years,
at least not its solid structure.
I'm saying good-bye to that house
and I feel good about new people
making its spaces their own.
It most definitely is time for that.
But I miss my family, all three.
Geof, whose bedroom and mine shared a wall,
who was diligent in his studies and his fitness,
who made sure that all his senior friends
helped out his freshman sister
at Waterville High the same year
as the kitchen remodel.
Dad, who tucked me in every night
in my little green bedroom,
listening to the tales of my day.
Mom, who took such joy in that
house being ours, hers,
and intrepidly maintained it
as home until she could no longer.
Once the four of us, now only me.
I miss them, each.
4 Roberts Avenue,
I'll miss you a bit, too.

July 12, 2020

# Above

When I fell on that bridge
and could not go on,
it was life-changing.
Like that bridge,
I've borne a load without question.
I'm realizing now that
my structure is magical, too.
That day, those moments
on the bridge with my friend,
opened me up
ever more deeply to me.
In pain, dizzy, breathless, unsure—
somehow I felt above it, too.
I knew there was more to it
than just the fall.
In the midst and, yet,
above the fray once again.
My body let me know
that I simply had to sit, wait,
let the in-between be.
I needed that lesson.
As the pain of my injuries slowly subsides,

I am reminded
that the things that matter
are not terribly complicated,
come naturally if we let them.
Love, Health, Connection,
Empathy, Trust, Peace.
All part of our make-up,
marvels of engineering that we are.
More evidence that in stopping
there is movement.
Like soft summer clouds
above gentle ocean waves,
accompanied by the whisper of a breeze
in the evergreen trees,
there is a freshening
to being neither here nor there,
in allowing time for suspension.

July 17, 2020

# Novel Ways to Shine

Evening waves lap onto shore
as loon calls echo.
Bullfrogs engage in deep debate
as I slowly settle
into night's slumber.

Morning light seeps ever so quietly
over the now-still pond,
rocky sentinel peeks
from behind and above
flowy clouds.
My eyes open,
heart soon follows,
mind drifts
to the decision of yesterday.
Only a day,
and I awaken to such newness.
I walk to the dock,
sit, watch the changing scene unfold.
I breathe … deeply,
allow it all in,
all out.
I feel the truth of me expand,
with a knowing that I did the right thing,
difficult though it was.
My own light will not diminish
because I had to let go—
for me.
In fact, I do believe that,
just as the sun makes its way
into each uniquely new day
and morning light widens,

I will find
novel ways to shine.

July 20, 2020

## Celestial Energy

She lays back,
feels the warmth of the sun
on her aching body.
She notices a healing energy
making its way all around
and through,
particularly in her hips
and core.
She absorbs, connects,
feels her fluidity rearrange.
At the very same time she wonders
how it can be true,
this sense of openness
and freedom from suffering,
even as discomfort is present.
Slowly she realizes that this
is yet another twist of the lens.

Just because one has been wounded,
witnessed and felt suffering,
learned to take on the distress of others
doesn't mean that is how it must be.
Her profound
sense of unity with the sun
is true and real.
As the pain from injuries sustained
in her tumble on the bridge
once again gains footing,
she understands that,
though it is valid,
she doesn't have to allow
perceptions anchored in her past
to be in play.
In fact,
she can use this experience
to continue to dilute their strength
more and more and more.
She smiles with a knowing that
all vessels below have the ability
to connect with,
reflect on,
celestial energy from above.
It's right there all the time.
She feels so grateful
for another lesson learned
along her way.

July 30, 2020

# In the Depths of You

You're no stranger to grief.
Widowed at 45,
you've slowly adjusted to that shock
with both grit and grace.
Maybe you wish you'd done a few things differently
after he died,
but that's because you now have the wisdom
that comes with being 63,
and from exploring your inner landscape,
courage, vigor, hope
ever present.
You thought you had mourned the loss
of your only brother so very long ago
and your father after that.
You understand the reasons
why there's more to do
because now you've lost
your intrepid, complex mother, too.
And you've cleaned out the house
where so very much happened,
found evidence of joys and sorrows,
confusion and clarity,

separateness and connection
from each phase of your childhood.
And then, of course,
there's the fact that you reluctantly
retired from a vocation that you love,
one that kept you grounded
through so very much.
So when they come,
those tears that burble and trickle,
or rush and gush,
or take your breath away
just before they erupt
from your depths,
it's okay.
Sit with them,
learn from them,
let them soothe and soften
as body and soul revive.
There's nothing wrong
in admitting to fatigue.
Allow yourself to rest, renew, mend.
You will find what fits in your now
as you continue to twist the lens,
recognize and embrace
the Divinity that also resides
in the depths of you.

August 2, 2020

# Pause

Soft, smooth waters slide
along her body
as a morning swim
revitalizes her being.
Genial clouds roll across familiar hills,
reflect in the spring-fed lake
that holds her body afloat.
She welcomes the enlivening
brought about by
physical momentum
in such a beautiful place.
At the very same time
she notices an underlying fatigue
that seems to come and go
without clear patterns.
A sort of fuzziness
within which she can't seem
to find clarity.
She takes a breath,
settles in once again
to the in-between.
Ah, there it is—

the suspension,
the pause.
Right there, right then,
she gets it.
She doesn't have to know
why or when or how or what.
She can miss their presence,
feel whatever goes along with that.
She can honor her own courage
and tenacity and accomplishment.
She can allow guilt
and wrongness and doubt
to let go.
She can and should simply,
at least for now,
let the pause be.

August 11, 2020

# The Closing, The Opening

The best teachers teach from the heart.
I know that to be true and now,
as I adjust to retirement,
I can more clearly
honor that within myself.
Not only did I teach from there,
I live from there, too.
Most teachers I know do.
We are not just bodies in a room,
though it seems, especially now,
that can be how we are treated, thought of.
Yesterday I closed on the sale
of my childhood home.
After the closing I went to order
a headstone for my mom
that will match the Veteran's stone
that my dad wanted for his grave.
The love of a daughter,
of this human,
was front and center all day long.
And that love included me.

When I returned to my own home,
my place of refuge,
I was greeted with
what felt like a cold-hearted letter
from the school district
where I have worked for over 30 years.
It informed me that my retirement letter,
written with care several weeks ago,
had been received,
with reminders to make sure
I turn in any school property
(which I already had),
and that my school email
will be deactivated so I should
'plan accordingly'.
I will admit that I had
fleeting moments of sadness,
which were gently replaced by
gratitude for my ability to teach,
recognition of my giving and receiving,
peace with my decision.
The closing of a home,
the closing of a career,
the opening of possibilities,
to places and spaces where I will not be
just a body in a room.
Thank you, Sarah,
for teaching from your heart.

August 15, 2020

## Thank You...

Hummingbird hovers by my kitchen window
as I attend to multi-faceted details
of my mother's estate.
I smile, unease settles
with remembering how she loved to
feed the birds in Waterville, at Sugarloaf,
by the lake.
Thank you, Mom.
Dragonfly lands next to my hand
as I rest by a rock
during a morning swim.
Memories stir of learning to row, sail,
navigate Great Pond
from my father,
dragonflies our welcome companions.
Thank you, Dad.
Morning breeze wafts through a window,
caresses my face
in moments of healing.
The same room where I noticed the breeze
and listened to the contented breath
of my soulmate

that last morning so long ago.
Thank you, Barry.
Sureness strengthens as I walk away
from my childhood home
without any need to look back.
I can hear my brother's words,
"It's not yours to carry, Sarah.
It's okay.
Let go."
Thank you, Geof.
Serendipitous winged one
visits near my deck.
I'm distracted, but Hawk makes sure
that I look up,
appreciate such moments
as I more and more let go fears
that were not, are not mine.
It is safe and good and right
to feel the fullness of me,
the divine nature of breath.
Thank you, Hawk.
Thank you …

August 21, 2020

## Ocean Dance

Feet sink into soft sand
partnered with a sense of solidity.
Slowly she scans the ocean,
allows her body to suspend
in its salty embrace.
Every part of her held,
awareness wide,
she is at once
here, there,
everywhere.
She surveys the surface
more closely,
watches the interplay
of wind and waves and light,
gently adjusts
to the cadence of immersion.
At times she ducks her head,
dives into the cresting whiteness,
frolics with a fresh, vibrant
awareness of inclusion.
At others she turns her back,
braces for impact,

embodies her innate strength and wisdom.
During the in-betweens
she relaxes ever more deeply into grace,
enjoys the absence of fear,
turns herself over to
the healing power
of this salty dance.

August 26, 2020

## A Subtle Shift

With deep, clear breaths
there's a potential to slide into
a slightly different tempo.
A subtle shift
that can feel so very good.
Like pedaling up a steep incline,
reaching a tableland,
slipping into that just-right gear
for cruising with easy freedom.
Or walking on a sunny beach
accompanied by ocean rhythms,
salty breezes,

playful shadow,
whole-body smile
on board.
Or playing with words on a page
as a means to reflect,
transmute
wounds to wellness,
concussive jolts to life lessons,
trauma to benefit.
Deep breaths
again and again and again,
whenever, wherever there is a need.
Reminders to appreciate
the pauses that present,
gratefully gather
the pleasure of such moments that,
even in the tension
of experiencing a pandemic
largely solo,
are there for one
to behold.

August 28, 2020

# Spread Your Light

You are amazing.
You stand
splendid and strong,
rooted and reliable,
majestic and magical.
You weather so much,
shed layers when necessary,
let debris tumble or slide away
and land where it may.
Sometimes storms ravage,
other times rains gently cleanse.
You are simply in
whatever is.
Best of all,
you quietly allow light
to enfold your nooks and crannies,
embrace every part of your
uniqueness.
At the very same time,
you spread your light,
the beauty of you,
to all who take time
to behold
and reflect.
A stately, steady reminder
to allow the light in,
let the light out,
enjoy moments when
the circuit
is complete.

September 11, 2020

# Deep Simplicity

All the way in,
you are there,
have always been.
I join you along the shores
of our serene lake.
We sit together as one,
realigning in full and novel ways
as ravels release once again.
I settle into our
comfortable connection,
feel the sturdiness of my craft.
That which once held fast,
gripped hard,
pulled tightly,
tenderly ripples away
in currents of quiet.
I breathe
and stretch
and fill.
I drift
without care
or concern.

I feel a happy glow
    as I recognize the
        deep simplicity of
            resting in the love
              that is you,
                  that is me.

September 23, 2020

## Peace in the Pieces

Healing takes time
    patience,
        courage,
            support,
                trust.
It is both easy and difficult,
pleasurable and painful,
simple and complex,
quick and slow.
Most importantly,
healing is truly revealing.

Like a multi-layered blossom
that has been ready and waiting
for the moment that is right,
when petals can open, stretch,
reach for the sun
without constraint.
Each one beautiful on its own,
even those with blemishes
or damage of any kind.
They all bond together
to create a truly miraculous whole.
This sense of opening leads to
appreciation for one's own bedrock,
though fissures and detritus
are present.
Rooted,
like that blossom,
one can open, stretch,
breathe,
gaze to reflective waters
rippled by soft winds in the
waning colors of dusk
and smile at the discovery
of peace
in the pieces …
each and every one of them
that make a body whole.

October 9, 2020

# My Brother's Stone

In a place where
five generations rest,
our parents' newly-set stones
right by yours more weathered,
I sit and sigh and cry.
They are mine,
these tears,
though I cry for them,
for you,
for what just could not be.
As time goes by, though,
they alter and lighten,
as though compassion
overflows my heart,
wraps me in
my own tenderness.
I raise my gaze
to the leaves of autumn
that sparkle
against a brilliant blue sky.
My shoulders relax,
heart settles,

spirit widens once again.
I rise from this perch
on my brother's stone,
move forward into my life,
carrying with me the love
we share
with less and less
despair.

October 15, 2020

## A Softness to This Day

Even in hard times,
or maybe especially so,
events happen that enlighten,
reaffirm,
encourage,
realign.
And, ah,
October 23, 2020
you were such a day.
One where grace and love
and new life

outweighed anything else.
One where the world felt covered
by a divine, downy blanket
under which we could all
nestle together,
though some of us were apart.
One that began with a
monumental shift
as a dear, sweet boy
made his way into
the loving arms
of his mom and his dad.
One where the soft ripples
of that event
had their beginnings
with the arrival of
Otto Elliott Risch.

Love, Oma
October 24, 2020

# The Adventure of Being Human

Mountains, though ever changing,
stand strong in the distance—
their peaks and slopes
repositories for cherished memories
and the promise of future escapades.
A soft evening sky
reflects in still waters,
causes us to, as well.
Peaceful beauty
simply
there for us to behold
together,
though well we know
the movement of fathoms,
each with our own deeps
that can stir and swirl.
Moments such as these
along the shore of a silver lake
help us once again understand
the validity and substance
of the spectrum
from sorrow to joy,

despair to love,
grief to faith
in shared Divinity.
All integral elements
in the adventure
of being human.

November 11, 2020

# Upheld

Your wholesome body curls
against my chest,
warms my heart with memories
of nurturing and loving and
mothering.
This time of holding,
beginning to know you,
is fresh, clear,
has no tangles.
It contains a pleasant,
fizzy energy of
transition,

              connection,
                   unbridled love.
   As if your heart and mine
         meld together,
    though our uniqueness is
          distinct and true.
    You, so tiny and pristine.
      Me, more weathered,
    with freshness of my own.
      This mingled newness
    liberates feelings that are
       almost beyond words.
          I am upheld
                as I uphold.
       And it's beautiful.

     November 17, 2020

# Widen

She looks closely,
so closely,
trying to find her way in,
                      out,
                            around,
and through.
When she loses her bearings,
feels adrift,
she knows the importance
of remembering
to raise her gaze
to the horizon,
let her vision
be less and less
skewed by the lenses
of those who would
not fully see.
Eventually her eyes refocus,
currents shift,
heart opens even more.
The buzzing energy
of imposed tension
dwindles
as the fuzzy warmth
of boundless love
widens.
Her shoulders straighten,
breath comes easily,
gaze drifts ever higher.
Eyes to the sky,
she smiles and
widens, too.

November 21, 2020

# Even a Little Bit of Light

Some of us have a hefty share
of trying times.
For the most part,
there's no real
rhyme or reason
to that.
It just is as it is.
Loss and times of grief
are simply part of being human.
And, when you live and love deeply,
there are just so very many feels.
As I've worked my way in
and around and through the
effects of my own dark times,
I can recognize
that I have this amazing way
of finding the good,
orienting to hope,
eventually glimpsing
even a little bit of light
no matter how dark

it may be.
I feel so very grateful
that I know this
about me.
It's an essential
part of my inner embers
that I need to kindle
right now.
I can do that for me.

November 23, 2020

## Years and Years of Tears

And so they come
from deep down in my depths.
I know it's healthy
to allow them to flow,
though some of them
have powerful currents
of anger
and I feel a bit afraid
of their fierceness.
I'm home alone,

though I believe
that the Divine is here
and there
and everywhere.
Trusting in the
pure benevolence
of that connection
is still fairly new,
especially in moments
of releasing indignation.
But the time is right,
conditions oddly favorable,
for years and years of tears
to overflow my tender heart.
And so I will do my best
to allow them without fear.
Anticipating the cleansing,
even now I look
for the light that I know
will eventually show.
I can feel my healing,
but this is hard …
and right now
it hurts.

November 25, 2020

# In the Waning

I awaken.
A soft blue sky
beckons
and I step out
into the clear, crisp air.
I breathe,
feel my self realign
and rebalance yet again.
There is an emptiness,
but it's not fully hollow.
In fact,
there's promise there.
I gaze to the horizon,
then higher.
The waning moon,
on its way to set,
is tickled by
bare branches
of sleepy treetops
bathed in the widening
morning light.
Ah, there it is …

in the waning
there is widening,
with plenty of light present
and in phases to come.
They will be as they are
and I can be
as I am.
Thank you Moon.
Thank you Sun.
I understand.

December 4, 2020

## Slow Motion

Fissures formed long ago,
crack more deeply
by forces of nature and
perhaps a
concussive blow.
Jagged pieces break loose,
tumble downward,
drop into flowing waters
that rise and fall

again and again.
The undeniable energy
of whitewater wildness
provides movement
and transformation.
Gentle waters allow for respite, recovery,
profoundly restorative moments
along the way.
This trajectory is both universal
and unique,
as wounding, weathering,
wellness flow.
And,
like sand on a sunny beach,
sometimes you just need
to sit for a bit,
allow for light to
surround,
reflect,
emanate.
Feel inherent Divinity
in the stillness,
let motion come
as it may.

December 14, 2020

## Solstice in the Wings

I feel the presence of your love,
though your absence
can be very large still.
Perhaps it's the many
challenges and changes
I've had to process
in the past several months
that has me missing you anew.
I walk to our river,
fill with memories
of the four of us
frolicking there
in every season.
A gentle combination
of sadness and hope
swirls and settles
as I realize
they have been
consistent companions
since your death,
hope usually the stronger
of the two.

As I return home,
I raise my eyes
to a crescent moon
cradled by branches
of a tree we planted together
when we first moved in.
Waxing and setting in the gloaming
with the Solstice in the wings.
Well, there it is …
Hope, Love,
and the promise of Light
win the day,
even in the uncertainty and isolation
of a global pandemic.

December 18, 2020

# The Vast Reaches of You

Engage in healing.
Lean into the truth
that surrounds,
permeates,
radiates.

Suspend in an expansive,
lively sea of love
as you disengage from the effects
of times and spaces
that were devoid of light.
Disempower them.
Let their tensions
loosen and release.
Rest in quiet currents
that support you gently
as you mend.
Allow your pieces
to rearrange as they will.
Let go the need
to direct.
Feel the fullness of your vigor,
the gleaming nature of you—
no longer dimmed
by impositions
that were not,
are not,
never should have been
yours.
Honor all you learned
from that which was dark
and the related shades of gray.
Look to the sky as
you feel your Health widen
more and more and more.
Stretch surely and steadily
into the vast reaches of you.

December 24, 2020

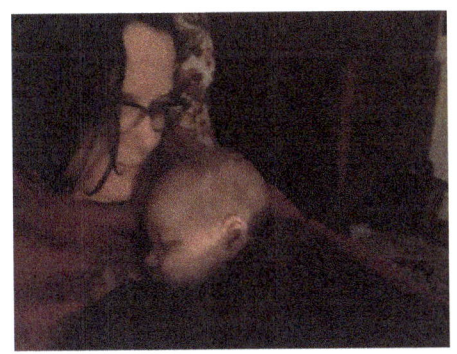

# Newness

No longer a newborn,
still he can curl up
and sleep soundly on my chest.
Every so often he stretches,
burrows his face,
makes those adorable sounds
that only babies can make.
How sweet it is to hold him close,
feel his full-on trust and love.
When I sit with him
I often think of you.
How you and I soaked in
similar moments with our babies,
both.
How much you would have
loved holding him.
Sometimes in quiet moments,
with him in my arms,
gentle tears come.
I miss you in novel ways,
though it has been so long
since I've felt your arms

around me.
The underlying emotions also
include a very large dose of joy.
So tonight, on yet another
New Year's Eve without you,
I honor the varied feelings
that ebb and flow
throughout my being.
I take a breath
and smile with thoughts
of our precious little grandson,
our wonderful daughter,
a mother.

December 31, 2020

# Singular

Being mostly alone
in a pandemic
allows one to alter
relationship within.
So many facets
to explore,

disentangle,
rearrange,
appreciate.
It's difficult,
can be so very lonely,
make you wonder
if you have been forgotten,
especially as day comes to an end,
dark of winter night approaches.
Wonders and worries sometimes swirl,
unanswered questions and
past confusions surface.
Yet, thoughts can be shifted
to brighter times
when there was a distinct
sense of belonging.
Feelings can be honored,
healing rekindled so that
tensions trickle away
with a sigh, a breath,
a settling
into the comfort
of one's beautiful,
singular
self.

January 6, 2021

# Such Illumination

The steady presence of the moon
has long been a fascination,
its nuances and beauty
there for the beholding
no matter what's
going on below.
All that is needed is
a clear-enough sky
and awareness.

Our beautiful moon carries truth.
The same side always faces us,
and yet the other exists.
It moves through its lovely phases
with varied amounts of reflected light,
but no matter what we see,
or even if we don't bother to look,
it is whole.
Its consistent orbit
provides the basis
for the months of our earthly year.
Its gravity pulls tides,

was probably a factor
in the stabilizing of the earth
so that life here can flourish.
And flourish we should,
even when times are challenging,
troubling, confusing.

The truth of the moon …
such illumination.
A template for
letting our own light shine,
especially as we feel unsure,
unnoticed, or even unseen.
Because just like the moon
we are whole,
we matter.

January 14, 2021

## The Energy of it All

As the effects of
bygone impositions
dissolve
bit by bit by bit,
I'm realizing that it's
the energy of it all
that is shifting now,
has been along the way.
It was a fearsome, frothy mix
that bubbled and oozed,
spread toxicity
in a stealthy, fluctuating fashion
around sweet, tender me.
It's in my power now
to let the toxicity
stream away.
Whether it cascades, gushes,
seeps, or dribbles
matters not
because it's just not mine,
never was.
As it goes

I have the opportunity
to more deeply experience
that which is mine.
I can pause,
raise my eyes
to the expansive sky,
feel the warmth
of the morning sun
around and through my body
as I bask in the
big, bold, brilliant
energy of me.

January 23, 2021

## What's True

This beautiful valley,
part of her life
since before she can remember.
This day,
though all appears
still and frozen,
full of movement and memories,

sensations and stories,
feelings and folklore
for her.
An eclectic mix swirls
around and through.
Heartache, hope,
anguish, adventure,
confusion, clarity
mingle
as energy within her
gently drifts.
She smiles sadly,
breathes deeply,
allows her being
to widen once again.
Though deep despair
is definitely present,
she senses currents
of comfort
as more and more
she trusts
what she knows
to be true.

February 9, 2021

# In the Glistening

Crisp air,
fresh snow,
rising sun,
strengthening body.
The power of movement
allows opportunity
for morning sparkles
to grace this
glorious life.
In the glistening,
facets of mourning
reflect and refract
so that healing happens,
despair dissolves,
spirit settles
just a little bit more.

February 9, 2021

# Thank you, Father

I took some runs
on our favorite trail
to ski together
so very long ago.
Timberline,
where we can gaze to the Whites,
appreciate our valley,
cruise the ridge line with ease.
I wasn't expecting you,
but the softness of the sky
seemed to descend,
wrap me in comfort and support
as I carved graceful arcs
in the twinkling snow.
Whispered words of gentle reminder
helped me connect to
ubiquitous love.
My whole body settled
into sensations of hope, ease,
security, and peace.
Thank you, Father.
I needed that so very much.

I will once again suspend
in these moments of
in-between,
as a stiff, shadowy unease
slowly and steadily melts,
eventually evaporates away.

February 14, 2021

## This Light of Mine

Good morning, Me.
I love how you rose up,
larger than life
on the trail ahead
just when I needed you.
Working through
a detached despair
that sloshes about,
my body was achy and weary.
But, I went skiing anyway,
knowing that
fresh air, forward momentum,

the company of trees,
were necessary.
As I was climbing,
so was the sun.
It peeked from behind me,
found an opening,
warmed my back,
allowed me to rise
in front of my self.
A quiet pause,
a gentle breath,
a dawning joy,
a deeper notion
that despite the heaviness
of details of the dark,
this light of mine
is good and strong
and so very right.

February 26, 2020

# Unbounded

The losses and stresses
of my young life
took a seat
way in the back
as I was obscured
by the needs of others.
Still, I know love when I feel it.
The brightness,
the rightness of my light
was surrounded,
almost encapsulated,
by dense, distressing darkness.
Still, it shines.
Often in my past
when I was hurting
or needing help,
I ran headlong
into a wall of anger and disdain.
Still, I find my way to healing.
I lost so much on a May day in 2002.
There one minute, gone the next.
Still, here I am—
tender, radiant, lively me.
Energetic, fun-loving,
go-out-for-a-ski-
even-though-it's-13-below-
giggle-at-frozen-eyelashes-
and-frosty-hair me.
I'm right here,
learning to relax into
the dawning joy
of being unbounded.

March 2, 2021

# A Pandemic Year Through the Heart of a Teacher

**Friday, March 13, 2020**
After a tense week
trying to appease the fears
of fourth grade minds and hearts,
she walks out the door
of her beloved classroom.
Little does she know
that she will never go back
to teaching as she had known it
for 30 years.
There begins a time
of losses and gains,
unease and sureness,
confusion and certainty,
and everything in between—
sometimes all at once.

**Saturday, March 13, 2021**
After a tense few days
appeasing the fears
of her own mind and heart,

she walks through a door opened
by science and leadership.
Emotions stirring,
she is met by volunteers
smiling behind masks,
gentle support in their eyes.
Joining a smooth flow
of veteran educators,
she is ushered into a large room
staffed by compassionate medical workers.
An explanation,
a pause for questions,
a quick jab
that she hardly feels,
a time to sit and make
sure her body accepts
the vaccine.
Taking a relieved and grateful breath,
she walks out another door,
hope and appreciation
filling her heart.

March 14, 2021

# Mommy...Where's God?

I sit uncomfortably
in a house of worship
that is not familiar to me,
my four-year-old son
in my lap.
He cranes his neck,
looks up at a large, ornate cross
hanging over an altar that
seems so very far away.
His sweet, innocent voice
reaches my ears with
a whisper,
"Mommy… where's God?"
His wonderful father,
my soulmate,
sits next to my shoulder
holding our
two-year-old daughter.
He turns to me with
a knowing smile,
blue eyes twinkling,
an unspoken question of,

"So, how will you answer that one,
my love?"
And, without missing more than
a few beats
I hug our precious son,
his blue eyes searching my face,
and say,
"God is here, and there,
and everywhere."
In that moment,
that answer is enough.
And we,
the four of us,
settle into the love
that binds us
just a little bit more.

March 22, 2021

# Moments Such as This

I walk familiar circles,
though inner dialogue shifts.
One foot in front of the other
as onward I move.
I hear your song,
but don't take notice
at first.
Your gentle persistence penetrates.
Upward I gaze,
locate you
on a branch
underlit by the morning sun,
clear blue sky your canvas.
I thank you for moments such as this.
I don't yet fully understand
and loneliness remains a constant,
though it wanes.
I will continue to listen
and look for these opportunities
to let go residual angst,
tap my steady wisdom,

build trust in my
connection
to you.

April 9, 2021

## Solace

One fierce event,
subliminal missives
over time,
a potent combination
of the two.
There's no concrete memory,
but clearly my body recollects
some sort of smothering
that left a multi-strand,
        intricately wound,
           tightly bound,
ball of hurt
deep within.
Ever so slowly,
bit by bit,
unwinding and release

have accompanied my healing.
Residual fury
sometimes kindles,
a valid part of the wound.
When I sit with the stillness
that comes after such a surge,
more deeply I feel my essence.
Like a distant mountain
whose familiar silhouette
brings solace in varied skies,
my inner world
more and more
a place of comfort
for me.

April 16, 2021

## Salty Softness

Spring winds gently swirl
as a lively ocean adjusts
to an incoming tide.
She walks slowly,
listens

both out and in.
Reminiscing,
    remembering,
        realigning.
She has no real plan
other than to be there,
see what comes,
relax in moments
of in-between.
She is drawn out
    along a sand bar,
        closer to the
            breaking waves.
Soothing ocean rhythms
bring tender tears
and she speaks her heart
to those who are gone.
She hears empathy
as she articulates her truth,
currents of self-compassion
now part of her flow.
She looks to the horizon,
sandwiched between briny waves
and velvety clouds.
She feels at once grounded and lofty,
smiles at the salty softness
of allowing.

April 22, 2021

# Finding Oneself in Solitude

Long stretches of time
alone
in the past year or so,
though challenging,
have allowed much to come
to light.
Unfettered recognition of
illusion,
pain,
strength,
truth.
Uneasy wonderings of
who remembers,
where to fit,
what is next,
when, how, if to re-emerge.
Sometimes so clear,
other times
just out of focus.
Branching moments
of suspension
create currents of

gratitude for love let in,
comfort in quiet company,
hope of candid connection.
Valid,
vital,
revealing,
redeeming—
finding oneself
in solitude.

May 2, 2021

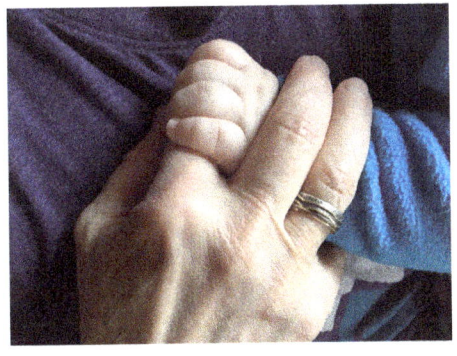

## I'll Hold You, Too

Unsettled,
you are in need
of comfort.
I speak quiet words
of encouragement
and love.
Slowly and steadily
your body relaxes
and you nestle
into my arms,

tiny fingers
wrapped around
one of mine.
Once again I drift back
to days of mothering.
Precious moments of
holding my babies,
calming their unease,
soothing their tears,
basking in wholesome love shared
with them and their sweet dad.
A tender sigh brings me
back to you,
your contented breath
and gentle holding.
I'm so very happy
that I get
to hold you, too.

May 9, 2021

# Smothered No Longer

The wounds of grief,
whatever the origin,
need not be fully defined
as dark,
though that does
loom large early on.
Given space
to express and honor,
explore and heal,
one gains the opening
to transmute.
There is potential
to access
diffusing Light,
branching awareness,
currents of quiet peace.
When grief bursts come now
I know what to do:
Allow,
speak,
cry,
remember,
love…
me.
Breathe,
ponder,
recover,
hold,
be …
me.
What sweet relief it is
to have my grief
smothered no longer.

What dawning joy
I uncover
by granting it
with Love.

May 14, 2021

# Held

Pencil in hand
I pause,
breathe, allow,
know to let words
simply flow as they may,
as they have so many times
over these past years.
Early on they came
in a quickening,
poured forth
as grief
opened the way.
More often now
there's a gentle tug and
they come in

peaceful currents
as images, perceptions
flicker
and flutter
until a clear reflection presents.
There's an enjoyable aspect
of wordplay
as my sweet wild child's
poetic purity
darts
and dances
until she feels heard.
When I write
I feel held,
buoyant,
limitless,
suspended.
Waters meet sky,
dark and light mingle,
and it matters not
who else might listen.

May 28, 2021

# The Fullness of Grief

As thoughts drift
back to what was,
there can be loneliness,
heartache,
longing.
So many of us were taught
to control our tears,
hide our despair,
that there is some sort of order
to grief.
All of that is fallacy.
Body may tighten,
breath restrict,
spirit become uneasy.
Yet, when the tension
of unexpressed sorrow unwinds,
when it is allowed to surface
and tears flow free,
one can experience
the fullness of grief.
This is uniquely individual,
can not be prescribed,

should not be judged.
Honor love shared,
comfort an aching soul,
reclaim and rejuvenate
one's sweet self.
Such is the
power and potential
of enabling
the fullness of grief.

June 6, 2021

## Ever More

Though facets are changing,
the way ahead somewhat hazy,
she is peaceful,
feeling both whole
and holy.
That last part is novel,
though it has been present
in her tenor all along.
She just couldn't quite
acknowledge it fully,

for her faith had been
smothered, too,
by others who once
loomed large.
She breathes,
courageously puts words
to her sense of holiness.
Surreptitious shadows
swirl and slide about,
but they do not,
can not,
find substance.
Less and less
it matters
why or where
or how they came,
as outward they go,
leaving the way
ever more open.
Relief unfurls
as she breathes
ever more freely.
She smiles a
whole-body smile
ever more broadly.
Self-compassion renews
as healing finds its way
ever more wholly.
She writes and
again feels held,
trusting that there
is ever more
to refresh,
record,
restore.

June 11, 2021

# Unburdened

What a heavy load
it can be
to lug the burdens
of others.
Layers and layers
form, fuse, tip,
merge, morph, split.
Bit by bit comes the dismantling.
Some slabs, though weathered,
have a stealthy strength,
even in the smaller chunks.
The jaggedness of feeling judged
can be present
when one allows vulnerabilities
to be exposed,
when one learned
to keep certain emotions
hidden away.
Little by little the load can lighten,
if one is supported
in laying it down
or casting it away.

A confusing crevice
forms when friends
seem to fall by the wayside,
especially in a pandemic,
and solitude takes on new meaning.
Step by step, however,
those who choose
to allow grief
have the opportunity
to rediscover being held,
even as complex tears flow.
For me,
I must remember
the hope that has run true
throughout.
I must trust that the
flowing of tears
will help clear the way to
whatever comes next.
Unburdened,
I will continue on
to discover ever more
in me.

June 16, 2021

# This Day

Wind whispers in diverse branches,
shadows flicker with passing clouds,
lush undergrowth thrives.
She walks pensively
along the clear path ahead,
allowing sensations to arise,
come and go as they may.
Ancillary sorrows,
remembered joys,
everything in between.
She pauses,
scans the woodsy scene,
sighs and smiles,
enables soft memories
of falling in love with
a kind-hearted,
blue-eyed,
gentle man
to billow and swirl.
That love,
that passion,
that partnership
remain true
as she forges on.
Warm sunlight,
playful shadows,
dancing trees,
courageous human.
This day,
like so many others,
she chooses to move forward

with the pulsating power
of Love
solidly on board.

June 30, 2021

# Freshening

A focus on attending to the pain
and needs of others
has long been my companion.
So deeply ingrained
that I tend to override my own,
yet I both hurt ... and need.
This antiquated habit
of putting myself last
sometimes constricts
my sense of allowing
the rhythm of healing
to move freely through.
But, it does anyway.
When I spiral softly
into another chasm
that needs attention

I can get confused,
think I must do something,
apologize,
or that I'm simply
supposed to hurt.
Eventually, though,
my breath joins
the wind in the trees,
the pulse of the ocean,
the vastness of the sky above.
I can smile,
say hello to new Health,
let pains release over time.
A freshening of companionship
in this vessel that is me,
I become more and more adept
at riding
the steady waters of healing,
letting them carry me along.

July 8, 2021

# The Me That He Sees

It comes in fits and starts,
this pleasant sense of drifting
to places where sediments have settled
and images are crystal clear.
The energy of it,
of me,
is pure and full of grace.
My heart no longer feels broken,
though there will always be a void.
I experience a wholeness
that includes the hollow
and all that has come from adjusting.
Obstacles and challenges,
both past and present,
disperse with the waves
or dissolve into the truth of me—
whatever serves me best.
In those moments
I flow with less restriction,
my soul settles
ever more deeply,
I find treasure in me.

My gentle smile widens within,
stretches beyond the horizon,
as I realize this is the me
that he saw all along,
that he sees
still.

July 23, 2021- August 2, 2021

## When the Doing is Done

Miles and miles pass.
Arduous, easy,
everything in between.
On the shore
of a wilderness lake,
aglow from
paddling with family,
setting up camp,
grandson snuggles,
a hearty meal by the campfire,
I climb into my waiting tent.
Lulled by diminishing wind,
lapping waves,

loon calls echoing,
I lay down to rest.
A sense of ease permeates,
my soul settles completely,
I seem to know myself
as never before.
I allow it to widen,
feel the intrinsic delight
of embracing pure Divine grace.
Back home
I revisit the comfort
of that sensation,
understand the impact
of recognizing
when the doing is done,
grasping that which makes
one feel
sheltered, connected,
sustained and loved.

August 7, 2021

# In the Company of Love

Sunset clouds roll
over surrounding hills
with quiet power
and beauty.
Rains diminish,
leaving them to
uncoil, expand, let go.
Silent swimmer slides
into the calm, golden water,
allows her body to be held.
She lays back, breathes, relaxes
as waters, sky,
radiant clouds,
blend into her being.
Quivery pains that surfaced
from a once stagnant abyss
swirl away slowly.
In moments of buoyancy
both clouds and sorrows
seem grateful that she knows
to attend and allow.
Innate resilience,
ubiquitous grace,
shifting waters of healing,
once again support and guide her.
She scans the sky,
realizes that often
the most intense sadness
keeps company
with pure, profound love.
In acknowledging one,
enabling the other,
aches ease,

soul settles,
and the light of Love
gleams brilliantly
through
it all.

August 20, 2021

## Bear Witness

A tree,
or part of it,
fell in the woods.
I know this
because I heard the crack
and the crash
as I hiked
on a trail that followed
a stream to a lovely gorge.
I paused, smiled with the memory
of wondering with my brother—
if a tree falls in the woods,
does it make a sound?
In this case the answer was

yes
because I was there
to witness it.
The woods were thick,
the gorge quite deep,
so I couldn't tell
how much of the tree fell
or where it landed.
As I looked into the chasm,
I spotted pieces of birch
starting to disperse
in the slow-flowing waters
below me.
I chose to watch for a while,
mesmerized by how each of the pieces
moved at their own pace
as they flowed to places unknown.
I felt honored to bear witness
to this change in the forest,
grateful yet again
for the many lessons
that Nature has to teach.

August 27, 2021

# Crisis - n. critical point, turning point, crossroads, watershed, moment of truth

I woke up this morning
with this word in my mind.
I believe I've reached
one in my healing.
I remember this happening
many years ago as I dealt with
issues connected to a toxic building.
I made it through that,
and this time I know I have
an ever-more-solid
foundation of health on board.
But, right now I think it important
to admit that sometimes I'm scared
and feel alone.
When that happens
it can be hard to imagine
how I can go on.
Yet, I know I will.
Partnered with wave after wave
of sadness
are currents of hope,

though harder to access right now.
Perhaps this is happening because I have time.
Retirement and this ongoing pandemic
have surely provided that.
I re-read my own poetry
and know it to be true.
I believe in all that has come from
exploring my depths.
So, I thought I'd write this one,
share these pivotal moments of truth
as I navigate this watershed,
fears and tears flowing free.
This is hard.
But, my vessel is still secure
and I trust that love will lead the way
through this murky disquiet
to calmer waters ahead.

September 3, 2021

# Reveal

They come close,
but don't quite overpower me,
these waves of sorrow.
They move this way and that,
make me feel heavy,
queasy, off balance.
My body aches,
mind wonders,
spirit wavers a bit.
Then I remember that
unease, insight, and freedom
often travel together.
I remind myself that the pain and angst
that are present right now
do not mean failure.
I turn to my strength
and the buoyancy of Health.
I observe the intricate aspects
of what is,
what was,
more closely
and notice the interplay

of dark and light,
the fluidity of transformation,
the transitory nature of it all.
I raise my eyes to the horizon,
notice the solidity of distant hills,
a hint of blue behind flowing clouds.
My body relaxes in moments of relief
as facets of healing once again reveal
the power of unconditional Love
experienced unconditionally.
Right now I do hurt deeply.
There's no use in denying it.
But I can see that in time
this, too,
will mend.

September 6, 2021

## This Bold Love

Reflected brilliance,
there for taking in,
letting out.
Bold and beautiful,
real and right,
this gleaming is
full and free
even if obscured
by storms,
fair-weather clouds,
or a lack of noticing.
Like the pull of the moon,
the energy of maternal love
is there
always.
Look,
listen,
feel,
believe.
Know that when you speak
of pain or sorrow
or healing or joy

you will not, can not
be rejected or negated.
Just as the sky caresses you,
waters support you,
wind breathes you,
the restorative power
of this bold love
runs true,
around and through you.
You have long known
how to extend it to others.
It's time now to allow it
all the way in
with ease.

September 2–10, 2021

# Thank You, Blue Heron

I've seen you so many times
this summer.
Skimming the surface
of a glassy lake
that held my body afloat,

soaring above me
with your amazing wings
spread wide,
strolling in the shallows
along a beach where I sat
chatting with a friend.
Unafraid,
you walked slowly
with quiet purpose.
Wings at rest,
head held high,
strength and sureness
emanating from your body.
I have learned that you represent
self-reflection,
diving into one's feelings
to discover the authenticity
of spiritual essence,
surfacing with a more balanced
sense of being.
I know this involves
dropping in again and again.
And that I surely have done.
Though the depths can be murky,
they do have much to teach.
In those grassy shallows
I think you were reminding me
of the importance of
enabling emergence,
feeling fullness within,
trusting connection
to that which holds
and surrounds us
each and every day.
Thank you, Heron.
I appreciate the nudge.

September 16, 2021

# Divinely They Dance

I rock you in my arms
as you rest quietly.
I feel the depth of your love,
freedom of your trust,
rhythm of your being.
My thoughts drift back
to the day we shared.
How you opened your arms,
beamed your smile,
from the moment of your waking.
How you picked up a twig,
a leaf, a blade of grass,
a piece of bark,
held each to the sky
in wonderment.
How your body adjusted
to the coolness of the lake
and you splashed and giggled
at the sights, sounds, sensations.
How you explored the cabin,
every cranny and nook,
finding your balance

as your side-steps
become walking,
whole-body smile
your consistent companion.
You don't have words yet,
but there is no need.
Your delight radiates,
like the light of the full moon
that rises in a darkened sky
as we cuddle.
Baby love,
so pure and true.
Maternal love,
that way, too.
Like shimmering moonbeams,
divinely they dance.

September 24, 2021

## Baptism by Nature

She walks alone through
autumn woods.
Water music accompanies

her quiet strides
along a stony brook.
A leaf catches her eye
and she stops, looks,
listens, ponders, feels.
She breathes,
dropping in ever deeper,
expanding outward
more and more and more.
Her chest and shoulders,
which still so often ache,
settle
and she feels aglow
with an energy
that is genuine and pure.
A soft mist moistens her face
as she descends the trail.
Innate strength,
beauty, nurture, love,
flow steadily within
as she once again
allows herself
to be enfolded by
natural surrounds.
Alone, yet not,
brightening faith
saturates, invigorates,
cradles her softly
anew.

October 14, 2021

# Wide-eyed Wonder

Having circled back
many times,
she finds her way
to vivid truth
and velvety comfort.
Circumstances that
entrenched
faulty, twisted learnings
happened to her,
not because of her.
Of that she is now sure.
Layers adjust
and reintegrate,
fears that were bestowed
evaporate.
She gazes aloft
with wide-eyed wonder,
glows with the grace of discovery,
fosters her sanctuary within.
She expands to the downy yonder,
feels reverential,
less troubled,

curious to experience
what else this
wonderment
might reveal.

October 15, 2021

# Of Sunshine and Raindrops

Things seem so clear at times.
At others they
are vague and murky.
I'm much more at ease
in me,
while at the same time
I'm uncertain as to
where I belong.
So I breathe and settle,
accept and allow,
stretch and widen.
And, sometimes I'm treated
to magical moments
such as a rainbow extending
from rocky cliffs to vibrant trees.

One that is so low to the ground
you can see through the layers
and it makes your breath catch
in that really good way.
And I realize
this vivid beacon
could only happen
with an ideal mix
of sunshine and raindrops.
I'm so very grateful
that I was in the right place
at the right time
so I could soak it in
with a quiet grin,
let the accompanying sensations
saturate and soothe
in whatever ways
they will.

October 22, 2021

# Collected Sorrow

Though I know I have felt hopeful
and grateful and joyful
all along my way,
I now understand
collected sorrow
has long been
a stealthy burden
and much of it
simply is not mine.
Some of it saturated deeply,
some beaded and pooled,
some already dripped away.
I think it will take a bit more time
to allow myself to let go
the responsibility,
to not feel as though
I'm falling short if
I choose to fully attend
to my authentic emotions,
whatever they may be.
What is truly imperative
is the recognition
that I've consistently acted
from a place of caring deeply,
being a helper,
wanting to create ease
for the ones I love.
This, however,
does not mean I must
absorb or carry
the despair of others,
causing unease
within me.

In truth, there is
nothing selfish
or nefarious
to that.

October 28, 2021

## **Because I Am In It**

As I re-read my poems
I waver between thinking
I keep saying the same thing,
to actual awe in how
keenly I articulate
the meanderings of healing.
As I see those words,
I know the latter to be true.
I have chosen to keep writing
through a global pandemic that, for me,
includes a wide range of life experiences,
from the death of a mother
to retirement from a beloved profession
to the birth of my first grandchild.
Through it all

my home has become a sanctuary,
though I think it may be time to move.
I was curious about those two thoughts
coming together in my mind.
As I returned from a walk just yesterday
I thought, "I love this space ... ohhhhh ...
I love this space
because I am in it."
Like a late-season rose,
I open to the changes within
and all around.
I'm not sure what is next,
but this meander has led me
right back
to me.
A pure, unfurled,
wonder-filled me,
aglow with appreciation
of my very own self.

November 10, 2021

# Led by Light

Some storms
can be seen approaching
as winds whirl,
darkenings roil.
Some contain
concussive blows
that strike without warning.
Others loom in the distance,
slide in slowly
as intricate energies uncoil.
Sometimes, though,
one can gaze to the horizon,
observe the potential,
feel the energy
without care
as to whether or not
thunder rumbles,
winds freshen,
rains fall.
Translucent, divergent tempests
coexist with a sparkling sense of being.
An opportunity to remember

and honor
the resilience and fortitude
with which stormy times
have been met,
how cleansing
wind and rain can be,
how the warming sun,
glowing moon,
twinkling stars,
are actually always there.
A chance
to more deeply fathom
that we are
surrounded by,
connected to,
led by Light.
A looking back
in the interest of
moving forward
into the peace
of an unlimited now.

November 24, 2021

# In and Around and Above

Oh, my goodness.
The goodness that is mine,
that is me.
How much you have endured.
How gently relentless
you have been in
looking,
listening,
learning
from all
you have explored.
As the sorrows you collected,
thought were yours to carry,
release and flow away,
your own sorrows
are asking to be heard.
It's okay.
You have the time
and the space
and the ability.
There's no reason
to feel guilty

                or selfish
          or wrong.
                Remember to let yourself
                be led by the light,
                    the love,
                    that is in
                   and around
                   and above.
                   It's safe to
                 all the way feel
                 your very own
                   pain, grief,
                   joy, truth.
                 Oh my goodness,
                    it's time.

              November 24, 2021

## The Calm Comfort of Love

            I can still see it—
          the blueness of your eyes,
          filled with love as they
               reflected me

back to me.
I can still feel it
as I did the same for you.
An interconnection
that was so deep and genuine
even during hard times,
maybe especially so.
It's what I miss the most,
when we would have teamed up,
been there for each other,
found our way through.
When I really slow down,
drop into
that serene place within,
I am able
to experience the warmth of it
expand to places
I can't even identify,
have no real need to.
It contains an eclectic mix
of truth and mystery.
Little by little I have
come to understand that
the comfort of your love
has been
and will be
there forever.
Like the goodness of me,
it is in and around and through—
earthly and celestial
with a divinity
that is safe and right to enfold.
May I,
may each and every one of us,
discern the calm comfort of Love.

December 9, 2021

# A Sense of Place Within

I sit alone on a hilltop,
gaze over the valley
we called home
together.
As a new year approaches
I feel a gentle longing
that has somehow become
a welcome friend.
This, the twentieth time
the calendar changes
without your hand on my shoulder,
your kiss on my cheek.
I close my eyes,
feel the winter sun warm my face,
hear the whisper of the wind
and the distant bells of a team of horses
as they work the land nearby.
I smile inwardly
with recent memories of
watching our sweet grandson
as he finds awe and joy
in just about everything.

My mind drifts back to raising
our children together,
seeing the very same in them.
I open my eyes,
notice the softness of the sky
above Mt. Blue.
I'm so grateful for
the time we had here together,
and that I know now
to wrap myself
in the downy comfort
of Love interwoven
as I cultivate
a thriving
sense of place
within.

December 31, 2021

# Step Into the Storm

Sometimes, not always,
there is reason
to step into a storm.
Only you will know when, if,
the time is right.
There's a sense of carefully
turning to
instead of away,
which can allow for
liberation of static tension
that may have been bound up
for a very long time.
It becomes dynamic,
with releases that are
both breath taking
and breath giving.
Sometimes in the midst
of a storm
one may feel lonely,
unsure,
even disoriented.
Take refuge if necessary.
Or pause,
remember,
notice,
allow.
Be still and
feel the sacred flow
of breath, health,
connection,
love.
Even prickly pine needles
may have downy blankets

before the winds of change stir.
Beauty and comfort only seen
by finding the courage
to step into the storm.

January 18, 2022

## **Anew**

I watch our sweet grandson
look here, there, everywhere
as he discovers his way
in this wonderful world.
My mind drifts back to our children
doing the same,
to times with my father
finding stories in the clouds,
to that special night by the river
as two geese provided
a divine moment that has
fortified me for almost 20 years.
I think of all the messages
from the natural world
that confirm or accentuate my healing,

make their way through
my mind and heart to these poems
I share with courage, hope, and love.
Though I know there is more
to mend, learn, write, share,
I offer some straightforward advice:
Please remember to pause, look, ponder—
in the midst of the storm,
during times of transition,
in the mundane moments
along the way.
Up, down, in, out.
Scan the horizon,
notice minutiae,
twist the lens
when the time is right.
None of us are strangers to heartache,
which is all the more reason
to let beauty,
such as a fleeting sunset sky,
bolster one's being
anew.

January 28, 2022

# Tender Light Softens, Still

Early morning
after a prolific winter storm.
I ski through familiar woods,
trees and trail
cloaked in fleecy snow
that sparkles underfoot.
Mellow morning sun
slowly warms the frosty air
as clouds gently disperse.
At the top of the ridge I
pause in the peace of the pines,
welcome the wisdom of the woods,
bathe in the benevolence
and beauty of it all
once again.
Tensions
of life in a pandemic lessen
as I turn to descend.
I let my skis fly,
enjoy a giggle that surfaces,
feel my self enliven.
My thoughts drift back to the days

just before COVID,
as we wondered what was coming.
I honor what we as a collective
have endured for almost two years.
I acknowledge
the grace with which I, myself,
move my way through—
grateful to be in a place
where hope often runs free,
the comfort of Love is present,
tender Light softens, still.

February 5, 2022

## A Hope-Finder

I stand in a familiar valley,
sensations of rich sadness
and vibrant health
somehow coexisting within.
I stop and breathe,
honor the tension of
that which seems
so diametrically opposed.

I gaze to the mountain
that has been part of my life
since before I can remember.
Such a mix of joy and sorrow
on its slopes and at its base.
I sigh.
A sad smile slowly widens
as I realize that through it all,
I have been a hope-finder,
an embracer and recorder
of oh-my-gosh moments.
Some of the tension
releases with a sweet gentleness.
There is a depth and a width
to that which goes,
partnered once again
with a recognition
of growth and healing.
The strength and sacredness
of the surrounds
allow for reorientation
to Divine truth,
enfolding the energy
of all inclusive Love.
Deeper, wider,
beautifully benign,
with hope and abundance that
is there for us all.

February 24, 2022

# Illumine

Ah, yes.
Here comes
the widening light
of late winter.
Its soft comfort reaches
that which had been,
or at least felt,
stiff and static
with an energy that
brings hope
and promise
and flow.
Sometimes when it
illumines
deep, dark places
there may be a lull
before loosening,
a need
to shade one's eyes
or even turn away
for time to adjust
to that which stirs.

When it feels right,
one can
appreciate the
dynamic interplay
of shadows and shimmers,
let relief and renewal
unfold as they will,
and come home
to oneself
yet again.

March 4-8, 2022

## Wake More Fully to Beauty

A settled being,
now restless with
a wanting to understand,
be understood,
in a situation that is static and stale.
A deep despair at a lack of success,
not knowing what else to do or say.
She opens her eyes to a dark house,
though she knows her light

to be true.
She gazes out the window
as the late winter sun slowly
makes its way through the darkness,
illuminates a surprising scene.
Drawn out the door,
she turns her face to the sky,
takes in the still softness
of an unexpected snow.
She smiles at the message
to wake more fully to beauty—
that which surrounds
and that which resides within.

March 16, 2022

## The Broken Can Blossom

My attention drifts out
the kitchen window
as I ponder an issue
I have been grappling with
for quite some time.
My body is a bit tense,

but my eyes are soft
as my focus is actually within.
Slowly, ever so slowly,
my awareness is captured
by a plant on the windowsill.
Not just any plant, though.
An orchid that had been cherished
by my mother
and hasn't bloomed since
her death almost two years ago.
There's a stem with several buds
and a branch, almost fully separated,
that bends around the back of the pot.
I turn it slowly,
breathe in deeply
as my eyes focus
on a blossom that had been
quietly seeking the sun
without my knowing.
A slow smile extends
throughout my being.
Ah yes,
the broken can blossom.
And when they do,
there is beauty that is
intricate and profound
and deeply genuine.
What a gift for all
who choose to see.

April 4, 2022

# The Quiet Beauty of You

Slow down…
Feel the energy
of an emerging sun,
awakening trees,
distant mountains,
warming waters.
Let awareness
of your sweet self
deepen and widen
as you reflect
and are reflected.
Inhale… draw in.
Exhale… be drawn out
for as many agains
as you need.
Let tension soften,
effort rest,
wonderings pause
for however long
they do.
Slow down even more…
Stand or sit or lay

in stillness
and see what comes,
what goes,
what settles anew.
No right,
no wrong,
no need to judge.
Stop, breathe,
allow yourself
to relax into
the quiet beauty
of you.

April 11, 2022

## Sacred Fog

As one drops in
and widens,
there can be a sense
of being in a sort of
sacred fog.
There is a softness here.
Though that which

once anchored
has altered,
there is safety, too.
Rhythmic waves
create a gentle harmony
that blends with breath and heart.
Vastness may not be visible,
yet is both discernible
and inclusive.
This sacred fog
can allow for
that which aches or tugs
or threatens
to disperse
as light once more
works its way
around and through
from above.

May 11, 2022

# Subtle Grandeur

One beautiful spring day,
20 years ago,
life changed dramatically.
Eventually I chose to
walk into the grief
of such a sudden loss.
There has been
both murkiness and clarity
along the way,
the path
filled with
challenges and shifts,
flowing tears,
and billowing joys.
I've landed
in a place where I can
honor the pain of loss,
the depth of love shared,
the person I have become.
Imperfectly perfect
just as I am,
I ground
to the accomplishments

all these years have contained.
I sit atop a mountain
precious grandson in my lap,
both our children nearby.
I breathe a contented sigh
as I look to mountain waves
that stretch
across the horizon.
Subtle grandeur that contains
stillness and movement,
grace and peace,
hope and promise,
and so very much love.

May 26, 2022

## The Power of Love

Taking an evening stroll
around our loop,
paddling to a favorite rock
on the shore of a quiet lake,
seeing a familiar twinkle
in the eyes of our grandson.

My thoughts circle back
to tender memories,
softly tinged with missing you,
that continue to hold so true.
Sacred fog may surround,
clouds may open
to the warmth of the sun
or the tenderness of
a glowing moon.
You are there, here
with us all.
The deep despair
of your passing
has slowly transformed
to a gentle grief.
Not a burden to carry,
more a sweet reminder
of the power of Love.
I felt it when we met,
through our lives together,
on the day you died.
I feel it still,
a constant source
as I continue to explore,
absorb,
and heal.

May 29-30, 2022

# As Wide as the Ocean

Decompress,
        restore,
      recover.
Feet held by cool sand,
legs awash in foamy brine,
  soul soothed by
      the sight,
        sound,
           sensations,
   of rhythmic waves
   as they
     swell,
       roll,
         crest,
            break,
        uprush,
     backwash,
    intermingle
over and over
and over again.
Shoulders back,
  heart open,

breath comes
with ease.
As wide as the ocean—
fully you,
fully me,
all the way in it
together.

May 29-30, 2022

## Fostering Hope

Such hard work
has lead to
a more clear, unobstructed
recognition of courage,
substance,
and truth
in me,
in the writing that
flows from my depths.
I am grateful that
grief and loss
steered me both inward

and outward.
I am in awe that,
though deeply wounded,
I found my way to
trust the path of healing
and its meanders.
I am comfortable expressing
an appreciation of the being
I am now,
have always been.
More and more
I treasure my essence
as it reveals delicate facets,
reflects the warmth of the mid-day sun,
resonates with the pulse of the ocean,
radiates love with the openness
of a wide-eyed child.
I find hope in me,
that fosters hope for
the world we live in
right here, right now.

July 7, 2022

# Out There

I look to the blue wideness,
feel the rhythm of the waves,
appreciate so much that
is good in my life.
I ponder how it can be
that one can feel so full
and so empty
at the very same time.
The fullness comes from
salty, sandy, joyful
beach time shared
with offspring
and offspring of offspring.
The emptiness is actually
small, but mighty.
Perhaps some of it comes from
the closing of a career,
saying good-bye to a mother and father,
solo pandemic time,
missing the one with whom
I would have processed all that.
No matter how hard I've tried

in the 20 years since he died,
I can't seem to find community
here where we lived.
This particular loneliness
is very real
and I feel right in naming it.
For so long, I thought it came
from something I
must have done wrong,
like grieve.
My healing has shown me
that simply isn't true.
So I look once again
to the blue wideness
and realize there's so much more …
                                      out there.
                                        And out there
includes me.

July 7, 2022

# Found

I stand on a beach
in the wildness of the wind.
Whitecaps crash on the breakwater,
sand and small stones stir at my feet.
Something stirs in me, too.
It doesn't feel good or bad.
I'm just aware.
I head into the lake,
swim straight into the wind,
honor the effort it takes
to keep my head above water.
I scan the surface as I swim,
break through the larger waves
with my hands,
let those less intense lift me
and let me back down.
I smile with a sense that I'm likely
the only human in or on the lake,
feel inherent vigor,
settle into a cadence that takes me far.
I rest on a familiar rock
where dragonflies often visit.

But, today even they
must be wary of the wind.
As I head back to the beach
the waves become propulsion,
a welcome shift in perspective.

A few days later,
that which had stirred
is unloosened.
A depth of loneliness is back
and I feel sort of lost
in swells of eclectic emotions.
And then I remember the waves,
both lake and ocean,
how when their rhythm is joined,
one is not lost,
but found.

July 11, 2020

# Quiet Currents

I slide quietly
off the dock
as sunlight slowly expands
into a cloud swaddled sky
and onto the barely rippled pond.
My feet leave the ground
and I rejoice
at the familiar comfort
of being buoyant and free.
I'm a bit achy
from a misstep that led
to a fall
just the evening before,
which enhances the freedom
and delight
even more.
I swim slowly,
soft waters
embrace my skin,
harmonize my body,
nurture my depths.
Quiet currents

of a summer morning
stir deep gratitude within.
Thank you…
to the Divine –
both in the wideness
and in me,
to the waters –
both of the lake,
and of me,
to me –
both in my body,
and in the wideness.
And,
to all beings who notice,
honor, allow –
I do, too.

July 29, 2022

# Remember

Ocean waves crest and roll
onto the beach where we stand
hand-in-hand.
Waters recede,
sand slides away
beneath our feet.
His tiny hand grips hard
and a gasp rushes forth.
I feel the energy of his fear,
pick him up in my arms,
gently let him know
we are safe
right there together.
I realize that something I have
experienced many times
is yet another first for him.
My awareness opens wide,
along with my heart,
and he slowly settles into

my loving care.
The ground did move,
it felt as if we were sinking.
Yet, solid we are
in our togetherness.
Thank you once again,
sweet Otto,
for helping me remember
the gentle goodness
of trusting in Love.

Oma
August 31, 2022

# Other Books by Sarah

*The Radiance of Change*  
by Sarah Carlson

*In The Currents of Quiet:*  
by Sarah Carlson

Available from:

DEVANEY, DOAK AND GARRETT BOOKSELLERS  
www.ddgbooks.com

SHERMAN'S MAINE COAST BOOK SHOPS  
www.shermans.com

www.ingramcontent.com/pod-product-compliance
Lightning Source LLC
Chambersburg PA
CBHW051058160426
43193CB00010B/1234